P9-DUQ-596

PLACEBO

EFFECTS

The National Poetry Series

The National Poetry Series was established in 1978 to ensure the publication of five collections of poetry annually through five participating publishers. The manuscripts are selected by five poets of national reputation. Publication is funded by James A. Michener, the Copernicus Society of America, Edward J. Piszek, the Lannan Foundation, and the Tiny Tiger Foundation.

1996 Competition Winners

Jeanne Marie Beaumont, *Placebo Effects*
Selected by William Matthews, published by W. W. Norton & Company

A. V. Christie, *Nine Skies*
Selected by Sandra McPherson, published by the University of Illinois Press

Jeff Clark, *The Little Door Slides Back*
Selected by Ray DiPalma, published by Sun & Moon Press

Barbara Cully, *The New Intimacy*
Selected by Carolyn Forché, published by Penguin Books

Mary Leader, *Red Signature*
Selected by Deborah Digges, published by Graywolf Press

PLACEBO

EFFECTS

p o e m s

Winner of the 1996 National Poetry Series

JEANNE MARIE BEAUMONT

W · W · Norton & Company

New York London

Copyright © 1997 by Jeanne Marie Beaumont

All rights reserved
Printed in the United States of America
First Edition

For information about permission to reproduce selections from this book,
write to Permissions, W. W. Norton & Company, Inc., 500 Fifth Avenue,
New York, NY 10110.

The text of this book is composed in 10.5/14 Electra with
the display set in Hoffman Roman
Desktop composition by Tom Ernst
Manufacturing by The Courier Companies, Inc.
Book design and art by Margaret M. Wagner

Library of Congress Cataloging-in-Publication Data
Beaumont, Jeanne Marie.
Placebo effects : poems / Jeanne Marie Beaumont.
     p.   cm.
ISBN 0-393-04128-X
I. Title.
PS3552.E2318P53   1997
811'.54—dc21   97-3978
CIP

W. W. Norton & Company, Inc., 500 Fifth Avenue, New York, NY 10110
http://www.wwnorton.com

W. W. Norton & Company Ltd., 10 Coptic Street, London WC1A 1PU

1 2 3 4 5 6 7 8 9 0

ACKNOWLEDGMENTS

Grateful acknowledgment is made to the following publications in which these poems (some in earlier versions) previously appeared:

Antioch Review: "Female Navigation (1818)" and "The First Red Place"
Boulevard: "St. One"
Caliban: "A Lesson"
Colorado Review: "Rorschach"
Denver Quarterly: "Sleeping in Your House" and "The Yellow Dress"
Gargoyle: "She Speaks from Experience" and "Photographing the Dolls"
Gettysburg Review: "Mr. Ripley Writes a Preface," "Mrs. Ripley Gets It Off Her Chest," and "Still"
Harper's: "Mr. Ripley Writes a Preface" and "Mrs. Ripley Gets It Off Her Chest," reprinted as "A Night at the Ripleys"
The Nation: "Arrangement"
New American Writing: "Visual Field Test"
Pivot: "Magic Carpet," "Domestic Diary," and "Road Trip"
Poetry: "Placebo Effects," "Barometrics," "Judging the Book by Its Cover," "My Demure," "Two Bowls," and "Pearl Hour"
Poetry East: "Vase"
Poetry Northwest: "Proxy"
Quarterly West: "Journey"
River City: "Childhood of the Invisible Woman"
Seneca Review: "The Others" and "The Last Blue Place"

"Visual Field Test" and "City" appeared in *The Denny Poems 1991–1992* and *The Denny Poems 1993–1994*, respectively.

CONTENTS

PLACEBO

EFFECTS

The Valley of My Attention

Fertile and   otherwise
terrain of rest   and discovery.
Place between   your outstretched legs
where you built   your first town—
train tracks from   toothpicks, mouse dung
footbridge of match   sticks and kitestring
making belief of   a stream . . .
There are folks   and folks there,
cardboard chimneys   smoke of pretend,
part in the middle   braid to each
side, a green   divide,
as I and   thou,
as   and.   The lay of
cattle-lowing   lowlands.
Where it all came   down to
when you'd gather   when you called.
Alps   Andes   AppalachiAns
Pyrenees Knees   Knuckles Breasts
Oh 'twere a   goodly position.
Prop the king   & queen for roof!
Those early   settlers
descended from   summit and cave
stacking up the   limber logs
in the shadows   of giants.
Here needs   formed a formula,
creeds created   an edifice.
You framed   yourself home
by the cool   well waters

where V   spread its valley,
red thread   could start a fire,
on the bed   where the household animals
curl up all night.   Tickle me there.

Placebo Effects

At first the tingling in the fingers diminished.
The ringing in the ears returned.

Early awakening
followed by miles of mental pacing

then the feet slipping into the slippers
waiting at bedside like two small boats.

The unmooring and drift
through currents of the night house. Unlit.

Unbreathing. The refrigerator opened
closed, opened—irresistible closet of winter.

What were the correct ingredients?
Across the courtyard,

hysterics of a neighbor's teakettle.
A light on. The early shift.

Sitting at a shadow of table
trying to pen down that last dream—

"a rat crossing a blouse spread round
an ironing board, snags it . . . "

That sinking feeling of being given
tablet A when tablet B held the cure.

No, the tingling had disappeared.
Back in bed, sleep would be found.

Snag—
Was this the active, the actual?

There was always something slightly suspicious
in a sandwich made by others.

So the reach for bread, cheese, mustard,
to assemble for oneself

what looks like a sandwich
in the charcoal light, what smells like,

tastes like one,
ergo, a fullness arrives.

The hallway calls—*Come,
I am easy to take.*

The mattress whispers,
I shall please you, please you.

Would the true bed be recognized
if delivered tomorrow

bearing its cargo of similar effects?
Don't tell a body

curved into a question mark,
sleeping the fool's sleep.

Magic Carpet

Let me tell how renovation beckoned
like an event the day the rug arrived,
and the drill and the hammer
were hushed at noon.
How we bent to the task,
unrolled it like a colossal tongue
thick with evidence not yet divulged.
How it extended the territory,
stretched room to roominess, a palette
of predominant calm with enough black
and blood red to arouse a drowsing eye.
How the floor clarified, spoken for at last.
How we lay on it like newborns,
followed the paired deer into floral thickets
letting the dyed wool fill our eyes,
suckers for intricacy, repetitions.
How it had been chosen not with taste
but hunger itself for the tale
the weaver works into each carpet.
How it would outlast us — woven to rove
through time, dwelling to dwelling,
and we one episode in its spectacle.
How we removed our shoes for the occasion —
my heel on a birdwing, your toe on a leaf—
and sank, so slightly, in.
Its fringe, thinner than fingers,
thicker than hair, waving along the margins—
hello, good-bye . . . hello . . .

Commerce

I am in the market.
The sad smell of cidering buzzes my nose.
I slacken the leash of my eyes
    and they roam from tent to tent.
Under glass, gold timepieces
    are unwinding their pasts.
Scarves of all nations flap on taut lines.
The market has been on this spot a long time.
A pyramid of oranges is old as Telemachus.
Balloons knocking heads stuffed with air
    from the colonies.
There's no telling what can be had here, even
    yourself.
Mementos.
Remnants.
The monkey who's hungry.
Eggplants purpling to no clear purpose.
Air is grease, spice, cellar, and field.
Currency has changed hands so often it's
    flimsy—if wind catches, it will be gone.
It turns to dust passing from vendee to vendor
    who squeezes it in his palms and makes small change.
All change is small but constant.
I am in the market
    for exquisite mint objects I desire I would pay dearly.
Remarkably, you're in the market too.
The longer we stay, the heavier our bags.
Heavy the air with smoke, bicker, hubbub, fleas.

Which came first, the one wanting eggs
            or the one selling chickens?
The woman with gold teeth laughs.
She has carpets unrolled and marked down to fly.
Free kittens, a bargain at twice the price.
A dealer of medicines waits in the market
            fingering liniments, tinctures, pomades.
You take lozenges that melt on your tongue
        saying *better.*
You get a discount for your disease.
I buy capsules to sleep like there's no tomorrow.
I wake in the market.
I'm in the market.
I can't recall who my enemy is.

City

*The catalogue of forms is endless: until every
shape has found its city, new cities will continue
to be born.* — ITALO CALVINO

Was it impossible to love the city
in which it happened?
City of unfinished structure,
city of developing forms.
Where the red crane against the blue sky
guided the calculated geometry of steel
through the delineating space.
The church sent blessings
and a parcel of its adjacent heaven.
The community assembled
a collective will of iron.
The courage to build slowly
in the determined Roman way —
to knock off at sundown,
return the next day and the next,
thermos of coffee snapped under
the metal dome of a lunch kit.
Already the neighbors' eyes
climbed like elevators,
passing the three floors of infancy,
ten of childhood, how many
teenaged stories . . .
Out of the great blasted hole —
which had shaken their bearing walls,
which had drilled them from sleep —
it reached, square upon square,
where all that could happen would happen,
faithful to the blueprint.

Ceilings, floors, membranes of the common walls.
Even feelings seemed less abstract
once the concrete was poured.
Rooms where they lost, pined, brooded,
listened to wonderful music,
wrote letters, washed,
concocted recipes of deficiency
or excess, shifted photos
of the living with the dead.
When had they moved in?
To what lease had they signed their assent?
Now, making out envelopes, they didn't
hesitate, writing the return address
as though it had always existed.
What began with desire, the girder,
the rising silhouette at twilight—
shape of things to come.

Visual Field Test

It's best to keep abreast of the periphery
    not by attention to peripheries
        but by a steadied gaze
            on this iris-sized black center dot
which could stand for global annihilation,
    imminent collapse of our system's sun,
        or your own small death
            blown out of proportion.
No matter.
    Whatever it takes to hold the eye,
        this focal point makes us
            difficult to sneak up on.

Head positioned in an artificial firmament
    the first light you detect
        is like a shooting star
            seen out your car's side window
while driving through one of the smaller states,
    the lone headlight of the oncoming night
        your reflexes work well enough
            to swerve free of,
or Corot's single luminous point
    that effects a coherent scene.
        Then it disappears—
            like the always finer light of elsewhere.

You wait in a mini-hemisphere of white.
This is the blank field underlying all we see—
strip away streets, clouds, shoulders,
bowls of pears . . .
and expose the screen for sight we're left with.
It is not nothing. It may be what God sees
and the next light (spot it!) from upper left
the sparrow falling in the west.

The corner of the eye
has an eye for beauty—
leaves pressed to a sidewalk grate
caught as a momentary mottled carpet,
that stranger at bar's end
who's glamorous
all the way around the room
until becoming ordinary at your elbow.

Look, departing your periphery now—
a jewel of light that blazes into mine,
so back-to-back we'd serve as perfect watch—
what escaped one would invade the other's retina
as seamlessly as night itself.
But meanwhile, someone is keeping track.
With each buzz of the button—"Yes, I see it"—
you fence your vision like a pasture plain.

That stud of light's become a fickle friend.
As it makes a beeline for that lone black iris,
it blinks out in an instant and is gone.
Doubt knocks and knocks. Have you failed?
No, there it is—reapproaching your center spot of focus
(lost lamb bleating into the barnyard),
having overcome the blind spot
fixed as Lucifer or love.

Barometrics

You would not question my judgment
if you understood the excellent assistance
I've been tapping into. Instrument
of rapturous subtlety, neoclassically tooled
and tuned. You ask, "Does it ever move?"
but I forgive you. I predict change
weighs in the air and weekend guests appear
like knives and spoons. The husbands are—fair.

I count this incremental way our climate's sewn.
Clocklike from afar, but tortoise to time's hare—
not even the hour hand makes gestures languid
as its indicator, thin as a haystack's needle.
I gauge the weather as a versatile material.
Today it's stormy, nautical as this ludicrous ship's wheel
design, and I intend to steer clear of the youngest.
I've been known to change my mind. You protest,
"What can it know of pressure, sealed in its glass dome?"
I've determined it is a bit inert, but working.

Watch—this swollen Sunday atmosphere will nudge them home.
Yes, it fluctuates. Not when anyone's looking.

Judging the Book by Its Cover

What feast is this
the neon-green limes advertise?
The forecast: hot. These peaches smart
like badly sunburnt rumps—
here is fruit to scorch your hand.
(Don't touch.) Berries heaped
in a see-through compote shape
a lipsticked mouth shut on secrets.
The melon's mouth is wider but split;
a knife wedged under its rind's back
spreads menace—seduction or foul play.
The spoon serves as cool companion
who undulates, reflects—
every crowd has one like this.

Look close, three tiny nymphs
frolic in frosted glass
on the fruitbowl's stem—winsome
hospitality, or mischievous? oblivious?—
under the bruise of dangling plum.

The night-dark noggins of grapes
huddle in the background
like bad seeds (who love company)
as a lone orange rises or sets
on a ragged horizon of gingersnaps.

Deep summer in the baking south —
the chosen fruits soften and sweeten and
sweat like desire, like this
enormous pitcher where lemon peels
cool into pale petals
in the iced tea we've been
thirsting for.

Contrariwise

I was supposed to eat the fruit first
but I wanted it after.

I wanted it later. In those days
there were guides for everything.

Beauty was no longer important
but got all the attention anyway.

Everyone wanted safe cars,
inflatable bumpers.

Everyone wanted immortality.
It was hard to keep (on) track.

How many glasses of water to drink
in a day, I kept losing count.

Whether I was supposed to march
in the parade or the counterparade.

Which pronouns to use and which
proper nouns were improper now.

I wanted to exercise
my right to live in an unsculpted body.

I asked those who came to free me
why they made me feel so oppressed.

Something terrible was rumored
to have occurred in my childhood

but I couldn't remember—
Was I the victim of buried memory?

Honestly, I couldn't figure out
what animal or car I would be if I were one.

I was counseled to plant seeds in the garden
but I let the birds eat them.

If I had to pay the price
I would dig into my wallet.

I was nostalgic for ashtrays,
leftover piles of peanut shells,

crumpled cocktail napkins,
a careless spillage of salt.

I invited the screamers for ice cream,
and left the doors unlocked.

If I held the door for you as you
held it for me, was I permitted to ask,

Shall we dance? I wanted to eat
the fruit after. I wanted to bask

in the sun. It was hard to make a habit
of premeditation, to say nothing of

meditation. How many hours a day
I longed to/should sleep, yet

wary of the free speech of dreams—
Pressing scotch in my hand,

one would say, "Down the hatch!"
and someone else, "Light?"

Frangipani

Here where first light rattles the bedding,
where the sun's wicked fist throws
its all-day punch and shadows
cut sharp as surgical instruments
so I move from one blindness
into another (the likely culprit
for my daily headaches), evening soothes.
The slo-mo clouds mulling southward
dark as a potion into night's ward
make the sky more interesting,
which is to say, it's something to watch
above those white eyes approaching, those
red ones going away—town's rush-hour exodus.
I find movement overhead
a comfort, this haphazard spread—
here drifts the head of a reclining god,
but before it can nod, it's decapitated,
cannibalized by darkness pouring over the mountain.

Things you might notice:
the prickly certainty of early stars,
the moon-rind moon grin,
a racket of crickets below the balcony.
My first day here I asked
"What is that smell?"
"You must mean the frangipani—
you can buy its perfume in town."

And over the hillside,
colors pungent as a fauve landscape.
Now I am inured to the scent, and that
skunky musky odor from the woods.
At first it was an affliction.

I've gone beyond the guidebook view,
outside the margins, as they say.
Yet what is an island but a place
with more borders, more edges?

This week news of you crept up
in a yellowed clipping, folded like a napkin —
your life story, with my conspicuous absence.
I imagine you drying out up north
while I'm exiled from island to island.
In my Pal Joeys all day,
scrambling eggs at 3 P.M., I am sluggish
as always. And I still keep plants
but not so sentimentally:
any requiring more than a weekly watering
quickly bite the dust.
Yesterday I found a young iguana
dining on flowers in a bush,
its tongue the sixth pink petal
scooping in five others — so much for
you are what you eat.

But nothing here would surprise you.
My painful attempts—to remove
the mind from the frame—
were your four years' exotic tortures,
or were they torches
held too near your beloved woodworkings?
Oh, this is my mouth running
from the island rum, a truth serum
for the distant and not to be believed.
It was long ago. I'm sure I apologized
though I forget doing so.
And I suppose I should thank you
for leaving me out,
for respecting my privacy,
that last, and best, resort.

She Speaks from Experience

Felt like I
was a word being
erased. Itched every which
way, brushed
aside, blown off.

Later, I turned
calm & blank or
never blank again.
A disinterested third party
who witnessed second thoughts.

The word love
can be erased
just as the words
suitcase or serene or
is there a difference?

In this book
were many such words,
a whole spectral language
to be reformulated.
Old rubbings.

But the rubber-tongued
could never utter them

without further diminishment
although they twisted with pleasure
& their intentions were pure.

A Lesson

I. Vocabulary

Soil is for planting in,
otherwise, dirt.
The donor is the third person
in the triangle.
Sty and style are not related;
neither are braid and bread
except in the bakery window
where they twist into temptation.

But some words like river and rival
surprisingly are, and more obviously,
void and avoid.

II. Multiple Choice

The woman on the bus has a _____ around her head.
    a. braid   b. style   c. void

The man who sells his sperm to pay for art school is a _____.
    a. river   b. donor   c. rival

Their child was taught to _____ the oven.
    a. rival   b. soil   c. avoid

She still liked to put her hands in the _____ .
   a. bread   b. dirt   c. river

The pigs, meanwhile, seem content in their _____ .
   a. style   b. sty   c. void

III. Conversationally Speaking

The river enriches the soil for planting.
The river is the donor of riches. The sty, however,
is full of dirt (the pigs might see this differently—
planting their feet, their snouts). The pig
is the ultimate donor of pork, which is to say
it has no rival. We avoid thinking of it this way.
We avoid the (thought of the) sty; hence the separation
from lunchmeat. We like better the smell
of bread (daily, given, whole) done up in the style
of a braid, pure product of the soil.
It is wise to avoid the void, which is nothing really
like the river, the sty, or the emptied bakery
window (its closest rival). Instead
we could relax by the river, picnic on meat
and bread, or just bread—pigtails are kin
to braids—since eating pork's gone out of style.

Vase

Symmetrical as a valentine
or the shoulders
of an attentive stance, a shape seen

against a wall, against a bright
window, against against.
What is so right in its lines

we recognize, though over and over
a different shape, the thing
as vase? In the eyes of the beholder

it satisfies the soul
like a sound body. A question mark
turned three-dimensional

or as the potter says—*thrown,*
some letting go in the process
that courts, coaxes, the ideated form.

No shape is normal, no size decreed.
Defined by suitability
for function: it must be able to hold

water, to contain. Once made,
that which is never empty but filled
with what we can or cannot see.

An inside sits, an outside waits, and vice versa.
You chose it for color or its ample
silhouette, now how will you call it—

a *vahs*, *vace*, or *vaze*, and what will you
fill it with, or whether or not—
and you thought it was going to be simple?

Arrangement

Perfection is terrible, it cannot have children.
— SYLVIA PLATH

In arranging flowers the trick
is to subdue the feuds
while keeping the conversation lively.

The florist bargains in bouquet assortments.
I try to find the common ground—
the schoolgirl collars of the daisies,
torch songs of the red tulips.

An infusion of baby's breath has been much
overused, but laurel provides a neutral zone
that is commendable if not profound.

How does anything know its kind?
The poodle wagging at the bloodhound.
I can bend this daylily and this iris

toward each other, this iris cut
from the cloth of night's first sky.
Is this perverse? I was told I'd make
a terrible mother and in fact I'm worse.

Snip the stems to get the correct
variation in their heights. A botanist could tell
relations at the cellular level,

what makes the flora
flora, not random impulse to design,
with respiration opposite of mine.

These hues were not created for my pleasure;
they had a mission. I traverse.
The challenge is to give each one its perfect
position in the arrangement

so they look like true kin
grinning for the camera at a family reunion,
a harmonious group in a dry universe.

Photographing the Dolls

I wanted to invent a record,
one worth filing in a historical museum
of the future age.
If there was light from the window,
I used that,
or if lamps were lit
lending golden tints of posterity, good, good.

I pursued true illusion—
a recreation where the fake
takes on the psychic heft of the past.
Through each nuance of position: head
tilt, glance sideways,
balance on a half-inch foot
                    —Look, I realize
they might all seem the same to you,
but I was schooled in subtle-
ties, out of fashion at the time as Latin
or home ec, which I skipped.
If you fail
                    to be charmed, it
matters little.
For myself I shod them, posed them,
shot them, exposed them.
From me they received books to read,
bouquets, a made bed, dessert.
I hung their walls with paper and pictures

and built them a room. Gave them friends
in abundance, conversations freeze-
framed for their tiny eternity.

Soon, a house. That is, many rooms.
The house made these words.

Childhood of the Invisible Woman

The child propped between two adults
    on a low stool
makes a bell with her brown dress
    spread around her
a bell from which the clapper
    has been severed.
She sits quietly, she is good
    all afternoon
as conversation floats over her—
    cartoon balloons.
So far, she fears balloons for their
    potential to
pop, for that suspense she will
    not handle them.
When she is given a cool drink
    she finishes,
even though something tastes
    funny to her.
To be polite, to ensure a
    pleasant visit,
to behave as though you scarcely
    exist. Is this
a memory worth savoring?
    Nevertheless
it is one that's kept warm on
    memory's stove—
the hassock fan churning
    summer-thick air

a velveteen ottoman, the lace
    trim on her dress
she will remember as though she waited
    years in that room
when after all, it was only
    one afternoon,
and doubtless, there were many other rooms,
    many other
more enjoyable afternoons.

Rorschach

Snow patches along the creek bank.
Too simple. Wings melting there.

The tops of two maples
beside the window of my childhood bedroom.

Stain on a linen napkin left by lip-
stick—why it's called that. *Go on.*

A man's tattered bow tie
put through the wash cycle—by accident.

A dress, haunted by the child who wore it,
standing by itself in the center of a room.

A face. *Whose?* A woman's face, lathered up
with soap except around the eyes.

A fluke. A *flute?* A fluke
with two eyes on one side of its head.

The cigarette ground into the floor
by Bette Davis in *All About Eve.*

Next. A house that can't be seen
from the road—no, what hides it.

Graffiti of the nearsighted
painted by mouth.

And if I say "tree"?
I'd say—death by wood.

Cabinet? Casket.
Tell me again.

A map. A map of the island
where I asked to be born.

Sleeping in Your House

Made me sad
          which made me unbearably happy.
Incessant clocktickery
      like a train passing over the tracks.
                (an old Seth Thomas, wanting repair)

      Hours trod up the stairs,
              thorough as termites—not one
                  minute left out—
      to tuck me in.
                      When I was young
      mother's "Don't forget your ticket"
              came before she closed the door.
      I had a jukebox of dreams
              and waited in the dark to find out
                  which the needle
                      would drop down on.
              (how autobiography replays itself)

I had longed to stretch out here
          and sleep between your lines.
Having plunged under the covers
      the night was my crisply opening
                  first edition.

Better than what I imagined (what you imagined).

I shifted among the you's and she's,
        an advocate of pronouns, how we embed
           ourselves in the text.
    I was mad about your
          handsome house of this and that.
             The pull was irresistible
like an invitation accepted before it arrives.

The hours of my best listening.

Your match lighting
        candle candle candle candle
—Kind porter!—
           across the rows of windows.
I, in my turn, and at my leisure,
    blew each one out.

Until the place grew dark enough for sleep.

Journey

I am trying to adjust to this perfume,
this chypre nuance; all day my skin
was humming floral notes as I was writing them
down "for posterity." All day I was wondering

if a woman could be kept in fragrance.
I worried I had let a journey out of the bottle,
that it would lead me to a desert isle,
that when I sent my message off in a bottle

it would wash up on still another desert isle.
This was my worst-case scenario, yet,
how should I define these passions? Which are mine?
Too heavy and they became their own gravity—

a body would sink under the weight of such scent.
So nuance. So notes.
But sufficient to the task, putting one foot
down in front of the other. Yes,

I saw my life as a journey, I said
yes, to grow, yes, to emerge.
Did I fit the demographics?
Did the scripted strategies make sense?

All the lyrics went like this:
If you go on a journey, it becomes a song.
Ah . . . if everybody could sing—

for Paul Schneider

Continuing City

. . . and they are still building it.
Eager beavers, earliest of birds.
Slamming wood that would wake us
from the dense woods of dream.
True, our limbs were restless—
we'd not slept as well
    as we'd dreamed we had.
Unstill. Until the crane alarms
like a parent cranky for destiny:
    you must get up, will grow this tall.

    What would it take to make us *happy?*
    the city asked.

Haphazard as memories,
how debris gets heaped—cinder blocks,
sand piles, great bales of wire.
A way to beam it all up?
File rough edges? Sentence loose bricks
to a life of law and order?
Here's to elevating stuff!

    (But would we know what to do
    with such happiness?)

How many nails to claw through the troposphere,
O skyscraper, cloudpoker, picker of blue
pockets, nibbler out of heaven's hand?

No doubt it's alive. Resembles the mother,
with its grandfather's height,
its sister's square feet. Night

falls, lights go on and they keep
on building. Drink in. *Drink up.*
Tomorrow the blocks of marble will arrive.

There are reasons why we cannot sleep.

More Raw Data

A woman dying in childbirth
in the twenties—one less
immigrant in Fishtown.

> The cap worn to signal
> the end of the affair.

> How a secret grows heavier
> the longer it is borne,
> one moment a jewel—

(This is your spine making a circle . . .)

> then a dull satchel of bricks.

The child punished for speaking
her parents' language
in the classroom.

> A woman entered saying
> "I destroyed every door I went through."

> So, no words, something vague
> as when lyrics are forgotten—
> *I'm feeling so   blue la da dee da* . . .

> [hidden, the way I heard it]

Is fear of sleep the fear of
interruption   or of going back?

A garment of grief was worn,
    night settling on the city walls,
        a shawl around the shoulders.

            "In almost any circumstance,
            they can preserve a wilting,
            diseased existence." (Orwell)

The daughter wanted something
of the mother's, a sash, a brooch,
a charm, one pretty thing.

                        Secrets are what is kept,
                            handed nothing else.

The father, courting new women,
gave everything away.

                A crowded bus existence—
                the taking on of the several,
                the letting off of the few.

                        frag / way / the / I /
                        it / found / ment / ed

Could we pinpoint
the end of childhood?

      . . . and every word is another patch
     of the motley . . .
         habitation in which
         I try to blend in

            (Look at your hands, it never
            looks bad to look at your hands.)

Sash / brooch

            I ferreted these facts by stealth
            digging at fortuitous moments until
            the subject was purposefully changed.

At ten, she was the oldest,
expected to pitch in.

            Things swing toward their ends
            with the weight of wrecking balls.

                One theory: the home was destroyed
                by the hidden.

. . . And who raised you?
Who cared for you then?

da da de dumm . . .

If I'd been told it
the rest of the story
would follow:

My hypothesis was set to boil.

But the clockwise churn of the blood,
the marigold's odd smell
in the loop of my fingers,

the urge to turn into
all these small rooms . . .

Proxy

You never notice my stare
or rearrangement of the furniture

but you know me; appointments
once or twice a week

have been penciled in,
my name on the classified list

of your next of kin. Follow
the compass of distress—

I'm at the horizon,
the illusion of a region where you end

and I begin. You know me
planted outside the cemetery gates

to make room for you.
The dearth of sky

where greed erects its avenues.
I was the fish too big

to be reeled into the boat.
The silence of fish.

And I wait up for you,
you fictional character you.

My hands on your cool shoulders
heavy as hands that have never

let go of anything.
Hands taking your measure,

rain lisping at your window
while you sleep in peace

because I am living
your nightmares.

Stratum Corneum

Once again, it is the dead that saves us,
this overlapping mantle
our bodies keep watch with all night.

Cell-sloughing sleepers, we toss in our beds,
beautiful, but—Beware—
microscopically toughened as toads.

By day even the fierce sun does not drain us,
our locked-in moisture thrives.
True believers, we handle the serpentine cords

of our silvern appliances without raising one hair.
Remove our dead and all doors would stand
open to shock:

like peeled oranges or grapes, we'd slide across
each other's membranes
mingling burning juices more than we could bear.

Instead we move smoothly in pure piled parchment.
Pressed against each other in this still night
we are dense volumes

from which old pages turn carefully yet constantly
toward each other—
far too many to ever be read.

Domestic Diary

Tonight, my parsimonious lover
—dicing the scallions and red pepper—
compliments the dangerous sharpness
of our Japanese paring knife.

Two days ago I whetted the blade:
circled it slowly clockwise twenty times
along a grizzly square of stone then
honed the second edge with three long strokes.

A restored blade is a fine achievement
for piles of well-chopped vegetables
season our all-evenings cuisine
and perennially delight this table's garden.

What do we find here? The soup spoons
stacked in the drawer like a year
of gibbous moons are once more tarnishing.
They no longer give our bent faces back to us.

We agree that the dull are loveless.
Monday they must be polished.

for Bob Mendelsohn

Gilt-edged Mirror

There's no one to blame.
You bounded down the stairs
to compose yourself in its story—
father straightening his gray felt hat
(when men wore hats),
your own small version of his ball chin.
That moment it began to yield something back.
Where I remembered it
the wall was cut out like a doorway,
so a swerve away from memory,
away from beloved childhood books,
to uncover a more direct approach.
What information could we do without?
Was its surface required in every room?
(Unlike a window, it couldn't be opened or shut.)
The view of a citizen who longed to
"do some good" settling for doing no wrong.
She appeared.
Like pavement, it gave an echo of each step.
Framing what failures, what pleasures.
A day you & he enclosed yourselves there
(love looking back)
trying to decide whose eyes were bluer.
When you kept rising from bed
to see how flushed you were,
observing each invisible alteration.
What swoon of pale flowers lifted you then?

Could one fit a square soul into its oval?
(Unlike an eye, it couldn't be shut or opened.)
The (best) intentions—to make the hallway seem longer,
to disguise the lack of windows.
"At the top of the stairs," I directed,
bounding up the stairs.
It hung like an ornamental hunger.
Within, the past gathered and restrung itself,
a façade of the future bred under wraps.
And we were nothing without each other.
I pushing again toward its shore,
splintering myself on the sun-worn oars,
and you always waiting
or, at least adrift
on the glass sea
whose eye was bluer.

Objects in the Eye Are Closer than They Appear

Something has shaken
me   i
finally know what a snow dome knows

. *small bits of debris*
in the fluid of the eye

dotting my eyes
minute lost boaters
shadows of penpoints   .
    pollen   heads of pins

cast on the retina

like breadcrumbs upon the waters
Alien visitations?
Too much reading?   *Floaters are most noticeable*
          .   *when looking at a light background*

Impromptu callers
   who enter without knocking
      who waltz without partners   .

There is no way to avoid the floaters

poppyseeds—popping in
when i'm under stress   *in most cases*
     . .   *floaters are harmless*
like gnats in the field

floaters often come and go

55

Do they shift like decimals
drift in orbits
shoot like stars   *change size and position . . .*

would i become blind
if i saw too many?
Should istayinthedark?   *or disappear altogether after a while*

This private precipitation—
clear out like a tropical squall?   *Some people must adjust*
                                     to seeing the spots

Small pioneers
stop wandering here—
                                     treatment is usually unnecessary

Settle yonder. Blanket my feet.
       Blank my page.

Road Trip

It was clear they had left the rain
behind. It was clearing, clouds
pulled out like old chair stuffing.
They had planned to speed past
familiar spots and dally in the foreign.
She longed for the intoxication
of each moment, but the mind,
wayward, summons whenever
whatever it wants. That worn
repertoire—how weary she'd grown
of the two masks dangling like two
wrinkled fruits within reach.
One laughed, one sobbed.
Certainly there had been more variation.
Good times, bad times—did they exist
or did the dilettante present
masquerade as the past?
Let's forget about the past,
she requests, so they can think
of nothing else. Passing zone,
trees, trees, trees, no passing zone,
then a yellow diamond sign
"Thickly Settled" predicts the way
though not in language they yet understand.
Fewer trees? Now she would reflect.
Miles behind it was raining.

Ahead night's Magic Marker blackens
an evening more a destination
than a block of time. The lane
shrinks to a keyhole at each horizon
where the car enters the mind
of the road like a new thought—
here they are—and then is gone,
where the blind follow the blind,
neither merry nor sad.

Found City

Designed by Con Ed and conned
by a million random switching fingers,
its constellations were what first
beguiled them, what spoke them down
from other miles. Down to a stand
of multiliths, irresistible variations
of vernacular forms, byways with motion,
the perpetual roar of motion, and
more lights—for here the day
was temporary and local.
Parading with keen purpose, great
aunts and lesser aunts, and youngsters
shouting Uncle, crying Mother,
and fathers, grander fathers,
widening circles of cousins, and the
not-yet-born kicking up a storm
all ready (don't ask). Denizens.
Citizens. Every creature with its story,
every story (should you inquire)
with a price. The old push/pull of story
seduced them. That and the stern green—
what must have been—goddess
enshrined on a nearby island with her own
bequest of light. It was this light
(for they were winged and not
unmothlike) or it was the liberty
nightly showered on the drifting,

part-time dreamers, the driven,
gifted, grieving, curious,
the crazed, the steady, oh the steadily
studious, the outrageously dressed,
deluxe assortment of this brand or kind.
When they had to leave,
they were sure to leave
a few of their own behind.

St. One

Most were unaware that one walked among them
the way they could become oblivious

to weather when preoccupied. One might be seen
standing in the doorway, the light at one's back,

a saint with a briefcase going about the business
of heaven—an apparition. There was a difficulty

people had with this. One, it was said, could not
be trusted. If one had a vision, lead should be

melted in one's eyes; if one spoke against
the state, one's tongue must be truncated.

This perpetuated one's trials. There was a movement
to subtract one, or worse, force one to have sex.

One thought it best under the circumstances
to take a vow of silence, to become a hermit

as many holy ones had done. This necessitated
the further grace of poverty, but how meager

one's needs. One persisted for many years,
though often the clever devil visited the cave

proffering sundry warm and subtle provocations.
If, in forty years, one misbehaved not once,

it was the soul bathed in light till it was blind,
the flesh bedded on stone till it became stone.

The Others

The folks who have turned around
in time are heading back
and bound to have it rough.
We just glimpse the backs of their heads
disappearing, gray hair into
gray morning, as we zoom by.
They start out wise, dismantling
nuclear weapons almost at once.
They call their planes down
and quiet the sky. Speed becomes vice.
They progress to the warm, curved
backs of horses, make worse time,
and study the stars.

    They rest by a stream,
telling tales to their children
of poison. They fish without fear.
At some point, the Forum
appears in their science fiction;
writers learn how to sing.
The discoverers return,
they've given back all the land.
Problems of sanitation
are reduced from a global
to a personal level.
This is viewed as an advance.
There are still poor.

Moving more and more slowly,
they remark, "Why does the ride home
always seem to take longer?"
Though they linger over landscapes
without wires, without one road,
existence again grows harsh.
Only a few at the end are left
to strike camp. Exhausted
and thinned they stumble at last
through the gates of a garden.
All the animals rush up
to greet them by name.

Excavation

What the water said   if the shoe fit

     whether the boat ever drifted to shore

        did the meek inherit   where the doorway led

when the end began   what only hairdressers

knew for sure   what burned in the fire

     who started it   how often it rained

        which grains were grown to ferment

          who bent to pick up the flowers

       what scent was left   flag remnants   jars

what dreaming meant   length of teeth

     where the buck stopped   ways to spell relief

       who said it first   who was buried in June

what shapes spoons were   the median rent

     what the wish was of who blew out the candles

who dimmed the lights   how long nights were

customs of tailors   how they carried their young

outdoor marketplaces   misguided beliefs

stars' names   coin shapes   which pets   which pox

who turned the woman's head   painted it turned

whether the neck was broken   what parts

were accident   free prizes from every box

what color   the day was

Mr. Ripley Writes a Preface

I have often been called a liar
which is music to my ears.
Who would believe

that fish climb trees, a flower
eats mice, a pound of feathers
weighs more than a pound of gold?

Truth is stranger than fiction;
my pictures are drawn
to that scale.

To answer the common question
"Where do you find all these things?"
Everywhere—

I never stop searching
for pearls to string
in the columns of newspapers . . .

the onion is a lily . . .
the man on the moon is upside down
in Argentina. Of course,

travel is an unfailing source.
In sixty-odd countries
the strangest thing of all was man.

No, there is no danger
of running out of material.
It gets easier every day.

Sometimes a reader is blinded.
I published a sentence
with all the letters of the alphabet:

John P. Brady gave me
a black walnut box
of quite a small size.

and believe it or not,
thirteen readers
failed to find the F.

Mrs. Ripley Gets It Off Her Chest

Let me say this, I believed in the bed
of nails, the man
with the transparent skin—

not you, though there were times
I could peer straight into you
and you never knew.

How did we begin? Your lips
brushing my ear one night, murmuring
"The hummingbird hums with its wings . . ."

In those days I loved everyone—
the mother of sixty-nine children,
the man who read with his tongue,
Shakespeare's illiterate daughter.

I wept for the people with two left hands,
the accomplished half-woman, all the rest,
perhaps too easily, looking back.

How odd your gifts were from the start—
a four-pound lemon, a handkerchief dyed
in a bug's black blood
—but I believed,

I learned to speak my part:
"The hummingbird's heart beats

a thousand times per minute . . . come
close to me for an isle of view."

I pressed your perfect hands
to my two breasts——Oh, how I long for
average things, ordinary news.

And I still do. Believe, that is,
though I am not here.
I am not here.

You're sure that's impossible
but it's strange and true.

Writ of Ritual

Beliefs were her den, shadowed.

Beliefs were hardened shadows.

Believe or wear dense shadows.

    Belief's where her tension showed—

    belief wore her down to shallows.

    (Be leaves where birds dance, shadowed.)

Beliefs were heartland shades—oh,

beliefs were hard debts she'd owed.

(Bellies swerve for dim sideshows.)

    Belief's words hurt and shattered.

    Believers heard in shadows.

    (Be leaves where herds and shad go.)

Beliefs were her tense, sad odes.

Bees lift, whir her, dance adieu.

Bees leave for their dense châteaus.

Still

It took five weeks to learn how not to flinch.
"Can you keep still?" he asked.
I said, "I need the money, so I will."
He drew a line around my body
like a homicide. "It's a cinch,
and there's a trick to it but I won't tell —
an element of fear enhances the show."

Circumspect, stepping down from the board
I'd look back at my outline
—legs, hair, shoulders, hands—
boundaries he'd marked: *Mine*, he'd think,
mine and *mine* and *mine*, a mental trick,
dividing the territory, staking his claim.
I knew the ritual.
Thank God he had a modicum of skill
and sense of humor (wore a scapular
of St. Sebastian beneath his satin shirt).
"Please be exact," I'd whisper at the start.
"Please stay intact," he'd mumble,
his back turned to the crowd.

No one knows I did this now.
I burned the flyers, left behind
the costumes with my worn perimeter
but I retained my calm interior —
with a calm interior

you can walk away without a scratch.
We parted friends.
"Thanks for the tact," I said.
"You saved the act," he replied,
and cast my life back in my hands.

My Demure

I doubt that anyone could exceed my technique,
and if I stand by the window and casually remark —
it's not the sun I love but its light,
the touch of light on skin, the way light paints
the trees a dozen greens and whites
and other shades the painter sees, you won't
appreciate the issue, accuse me of oblique
distinctions that are irrelevant to the point
of our relations. It's that touch that expects
nothing in return, like when we touch our own
bodies and know just what our intentions are.
Your alighting hands have motives far less clear.
See how I sit, legs comfortably crossed, my antique
bracelets quieted on my soft wrist.
I know just how soft it is and I know its
exact width and where the pulse tap can be found.
Having cast your eyes along the grounds I've let
you see, you presume there is more. You infer
my demure speech is just an act and set your sights
on what I haven't yet divulged. But I might not
stoop to perform this scene with such an amateur.

Female Navigation (1818)

As if she'd said, *Please burn the letters*
As a way of heating things up.

Or as if she'd thought, *Don't leave a mark*
As a way of drawing a mark.

And for what? She trudged on
Following, as he said, in his footsteps—

Twenty miles and a pinch of snuff?
His trembling as he told of the one room,

All the dark doorways leading from it?
—And, how to comfort without seduction . . .

They stopped in a sheepherder's cottage,
Stood their boots side by side on the hearth.

An old woman spoke, "You can read a person's
Fortune by how they wear out their shoes."

They ate oatcakes with whisky that tasted
Of smoke. She looked.

His was a clouds-to-sunshine disturbance
Like the two poles of his world.

She thought "smitten." He'd said "broken."
(He was never really at ease with women.)

As if she'd stated, *I'll follow you*
As a way of taking the lead.

One hundred miles into Scotland,
He said he wanted to compose without "the fever."

She said her bird always fell silent
When its cage was covered, fooled into night.

One hundred and thirty-five
And a fine claret was as good as a blanket.

. . . "Not that I'm not glad to have you along."
She recognized the spot.

The road dipped, crossing a small stream
With a white house hard by it.

And if she said, "Here I turn right,
You go left" and he heard wrong,

She still promised to come back for him.

The Yellow Dress

How long or how long ago I sat
   in that yellow dress,
not knowing my own mind by half
    but like a room fitted out with its best smile.

I was drawing his attention.
It was the attention more than the person.
Here is my hand. Here is my mouth.

Color me fickle then and full
of reminiscences, of women in dresses
  —awfully bright—good optimistic ones,
    a field of buttercups
       toasting the troops good-bye.
(Didn't everyone love butter
    by the bulbs of their chins,
       wasn't every one led? Small
lampshades inverted in the grass, up-
    side down skirts.
Soft skin there. Under the chin.
    O gold it was——oh, lit from within . . .)

I'd waved so-long, too, and waited.
Waved with these hands, restless,
   young because I was young,
featherweight on the featherbed,
    a breezy whatevertheless.

Attired in the color of my readiness,
I looked cheery. No visible cracks.

He was drawing my attention.
    The dress fluttered out like caution in the wind.
"Don't pour your heart out to me . . . "
He drew, showing what I knew before I knew I knew
    (come and go, come and go . . .)
How I lacked the palate for constancy —
Loving the teapots more than the tea.

Two Bowls

The Fish Speak

We trace an interior
    within the interior,
a room of water
    inside a room of air.

Goblet-bound
    we drink and binge.
We are not dainty.
    We are never bored.

Clockwise, clockwise,
    much to see:
green spades and spears
    held by the plants,
a busy wallpaper,
    our pebbly floor,
each other and
    our own reflections
(which are which?
    how many *are* we?),

a woman restless
    in a wrinkled robe.
When she leans near
    she is our cloud.

The Woman Speaks

I am a warm room
    within a cool room.
A reposing figure,
    a looking out.

How remote he seemed
    and I said so.
Was that unwise?
    (I am often clumsy.)

I've shifted the heavy
    curtain of flowers.
Morning ripens
    and makes its rounds.
From here I catch
    a branch's brushwork,
the road he left by
    twists out the square.
The light, blue-white,
    shellacs the table.

This shadow's more real
    than its bowl
or the fruit in it.

The First Red Place

Lost one, glimpses of your paradise
    everywhere—just today a woman
    boarding the bus with a floral-pattern skirt . . .
meanwhile, myself somewhat in shambles,
    shifting in certain corners,
    before favorite windows,
sure to be shuttering light in and out
    as though control could be donned
    and shed like a scarf/not-scarf episode.
Remember, you kept drawing me *there*—
    on the outside looking in and the inside
    looking out, dangling like an asterisk.

It's the exaggerations of memory that intensify
    its tastes, the sweet and bitter that
    lift me out of most days' blandnesses.
The older I get the more formidable their shelf life.

    I was the girl holding the book,
        the woman who continued to read.
        The gray eaves pressed in,
    forcing us to gather in the middle of the room.
        What was your invitation
        but one to dance in the book of fire?

You knew me too well.
I was the shilly-shally queen before we met,
a shrugging and short-spoken *she*
who just wanted to get home before the rain.

I didn't want the shot of sherry in the glass,
anyone shattering the glass,
pushing a shim between what I was
and what I would become.

But there you shimmer, cool
in the morning shadows of the terrace,
turning toward me—long years of you—
like sheet music as I open the door,
the warning notes of your eyes, shrill as ever,
wanting to disturb my day.

The Last Blue Place

The ghost of your last flowers
still floats over the earthenware vase—
gray haze above its flesh tone
like a cloud from November's mouth.

Sometimes this sill is stage to me,
to age here listening by the window
like a long wait in the wings,
with memory itself as tonic for disappearance.

Never did I shrink from the bitter remedy
of those blue walls, their company
in which I reclined for hours of hours
watching the shaft of light's slow

shift, like butter melting in a pan.
When the penny-colored fish circled
I made-believe an angel
had dipped down to stir the water.

The way you stirred up that blue.
The way the blue room took shape
like the hotel's Egyptian pool,
then the figure took shape—

swimming-not-drowning, or sleeping-not-
dreaming, a body I would step into
even now (entering the blue, entering
the woman's body) to have my hair brushed

one more time, to be readied for
my remarkable third-act cure.

Pearl Hour

Late spring's late sun
bounds off the white sill

to a woman lounging alone
on a mohair loveseat.

Her book's pages overbrighten,
ink blurs. It could be

another year, another era
in which this pin of pearl

and pale blue stone
was handed down,

the collar of her blouse
cutworked by living hands,

a scene where pages are unturned,
temporary immortality

pools like a mirage.
Now pause.

Little fault can be found with the sun
except its will to back down.

A hand reaches to the switch
of the magnanimous lamp,

words quicken again
under a hundred soft watts.

NOTES

Some of the poems incorporate phrases found in the following source material:

"Journey": Introductory package for *Journey* perfume sample, Esse Perfume Company, San Francisco, California, n.d.

"Objects in the Eye . . .": Online consumer health information, "Spots and Floaters." A product of National Health Enhancement Systems, Inc., Phoenix, Arizona, 1993.

"Mr. Ripley . . ." and "Mrs. Ripley . . .": *The Omnibus Believe It or Not! A Modern Book of Wonders, Miracles, Freaks, Monstrosities and almost-Impossibilities, Written, Illustrated and Proved* by Robert L. Ripley. C. Arthur Pearson, Ltd., St. Albans, Great Britain, n.d.

"Female Navigation (1818)": *The Life and Letters of John Keats*, by Lord Houghton, first published in 1848, reprinted 1946 by J. M. Dent & Sons Ltd., London as No. 801 of "Everyman's Library."